EASTER
AND
ITS CUSTOMS

EASTER

AND

ITS CUSTOMS

A Brief Study by
CHRISTINA HOLE

Illustrated by
T. EVERY-CLAYTON

M. BARROWS AND COMPANY, INC.
New York   *1961*

1237965

Contents

Contents

1

Eastertide

EASTER DAY, the Feast of the Resurrection of Our Lord, is the greatest of all the festivals of the Christian Church, and is almost certainly the one that has been longest observed. If in the early centuries there was some doubt about the date of the Nativity, there was none about that of the Resurrection, because that stupendous event took place at the time of the Jewish Passover, and was part of the personal experience of the Apostles and the first disciples. There can never have been a time when its anniversary was not honored by every Jewish and Gentile convert; and we know that, when St. Paul was preaching and writing to the small scattered communities which then constituted all Christendom, it was already being celebrated as the supreme Holy Day.

Nevertheless, in those first years it was not kept everywhere on the same day. Because Christ died and rose again during the Passover period, many observed Easter on that festival, keeping the Passover as their ancestors had done before them, but seeing it now illuminated by a new and different Light. Others, especially the Gentiles of the western communities, kept it on the Sunday following, remembering that it was on the morning after the Sabbath, "the first day of the week," that Mary Magdalen saw her risen Lord in the dawnlit garden, and thought He was the gardener. This difference of custom continued for a long time, and eventually resulted in serious controversies between the Churches of the East and West. In A.D. 325, the Council of Nicaea ruled that the festival should be celebrated, not on the Passover which might fall on any day of the week, but on the Sunday following the first full moon after (or on) the Vernal Equinox, that Equinox being deemed to occur always on March 21st; and that if the moon happened to be full on a Sunday, then Easter Day should be the Sunday after. Thus it is that throughout Western Christendom still the great religious feast of spiritual hope fulfilled is governed in its date by the spring moon, and can never be earlier than March 22nd or later than April 25th.

Because of these confusions, and the inaccuracies of early calendars, we do not now know on what precise date the first Easter Day fell, nor whether it came in April or late March. But it was in spring, in the season of new life and revival when, from time immemorial, the pagan peoples of Europe and Asia held their Spring Festivals, re-enacting ancient regeneration myths and performing magical and religious ceremonies to make the crops grow and prosper. Vernal Mysteries, like those of Tammuz and Osiris and Adonis, flourished in the Mediterranean world when Our Lord lived and moved in it, and farther north and east there were others, less well-known but no less vividly alive. Inevitably, some of their cherished rites and symbols were carried forward into the Easter customs of the new dispensation. Many of them have survived into our own day, unchanged because of their timeless and universal nature, yet subtly altered in their new surroundings to bear a Christian significance.

Easter eggs, for instance, are deeply rooted in pagan antiquity, and so are our hot cross buns and the Easter Hare. The cheerful custom known as Lifting, which has only died out comparatively recently in England, was magical in origin, though in later times it was thought to represent Christ's rising from the tomb. In Hungary, the traditional battles between Prince Cibere and King Bone now typify the strict Lenten fast and its joyous ending; but they may well be a survival of that pre-Christian ritual, found in many countries and in many forms, whereby Winter was defeated and driven out. Prince Cibere is a straw-and-rag figure, who fights the good King Bone on Shrove Tuesday and overcomes him. While Cibere reigns, all go hungry, but on Palm Sunday there is another battle, and this time King Bone is victorious. The vanquished Prince is carried round the village by singing, shouting crowds, and is then burnt, or drowned, or thrown over the parish boundary. With him, in popular belief, go hunger, illness, personal sorrows, and the dangers of hail and storm. In earlier times, this victory seems to have been achieved, more appropriately, at Easter, the true end of the fast.

The Bavarian custom of Burning the Easter Man on Holy Saturday seems to have the same underlying meaning. A rough straw figure is bound on to a tall cross, like a crucified man, and set alight with New Fire brought from the church. On Easter Monday, the ashes are collected and scattered over the fields to make them fruitful. In some other parts of Germany, bonfires are lit on the same night in churchyards or on hill tops.

Young people dance round them, sing Easter hymns, and sometimes leap over the embers for luck; and in certain districts, boys snatch flaming brands from the fires and run through the fields with them to fertilize the soil and bring good luck to the farms.

Even our English name for the festival seems to show heathen traces, for the Venerable Bede tells us that it is derived from Eastre (or Eostre), a northern Goddess of Spring and the Dawn, whose principal celebrations were held about the time of the Vernal Equinox. The Anglo-Saxons gave her name to April, which they called Eastur-monath. There is, however, another theory which suggests that the word comes from *oster*, to rise. The French name, *Pâques*, the Spanish and Italian *Pascua* or *Pasqua*, Dutch *Paach* and Swedish *Pask* all look backwards to the Jewish Passover, coming through Greek and Latin forms from a Hebrew word, *pesach*, meaning Passover. Our own English "paschal," applied to Easter ceremonies and the spring moon, has the same root, and so has the homely north-country name of "pace-eggs" for Easter eggs.

Easter itself and the days on either side of it, which we call Eastertide, come in the season of bursting blossom and greenery, when the churches are filled with white lilies and narcissi, and decked with the deep green of yew branches, which belong to Easter and to no other feast. But their roots are much farther back in the year, when the ground is still hard with frost or white with snow and only the snowdrop and the aconite have had the courage to appear. The full ecclesiastical Easter cycle runs from Septuagesima Sunday, which may be as early as January, to Whitsun Eve, which sometimes falls as late as June, and so taking one year with another, may span almost the whole of the period when Earth is spinning round from winter to summer. It takes in Lent and Holy Week, Palm Sunday and Good Friday, and runs onwards to the end of Our Lord's earthly ministry on Ascension Day, and so to Whitsun Eve. It is impossible to understand fully the place that Easter holds in the secular as well as the religious customs of countless peoples, unless we first glance at these earlier anniversaries; and since it is chiefly the traditional observances of ordinary people with which we are concerned here, let us begin with Shrovetide, the season of Carnival, of pancakes and time-honored games, and of that "last fling" which precedes the forty-day austerities of Lent.

2

Shrovetide

SHROVETIDE is the English name for the last three or four days before the beginning of Lent, including Egg Saturday, Quinquagesima Sunday, Collop Monday, and Shrove Tuesday. This is still the season of high Carnival in many European countries, and in earlier times, when the Lenten fast was far more rigorous than it is now, it was celebrated almost everywhere by wild revelries, games, sports, dances, and riotous antics. Food that could not be eaten during the fast was cleared up in a series of feasts and hearty meals. Children went about "lent-crocking," demanding gifts of eggs or meat, and hurling broken crockery at the doors of those who refused them.

13

Young men played a wild kind of football through the streets, as they still do in some English towns; and in Cornwall, boys celebrated Nickanan Night, or Shrove Monday, by removing and hiding gates and doorknockers, and running off with whatever brooms, rakes, pails, and other pieces of portable property the householders had neglected to lock away beforehand.

Cockfighting was a traditional sport of the season, both for adults and children. Fitzstephen, writing in the twelfth century, tells us that "yearly at Shrove-tide the boys of every school bring fighting-cocks to their masters, and all the forenoon is spent at school, to see these cocks fight together." As late as the beginning of last century, a fee called the Cock-Penny was paid by scholars to the schoolmaster, so that he could buy birds for this purpose. Cockfighting is, of course, illegal now; and so, happily, are some other brutal Shrovetide pastimes, like "thrashing the hen" and throwing at tethered cocks, which were once all too popular in towns and villages alike. There were also hurling matches, wrestling, horse races, and games like Tip-Cat and Prison Bars; and everywhere outbreaks of mischievous pranks and practical jokes were tolerated because this was Shrovetide, the time of the "last fling" before the unwonted quiet of Lent closed down on a penitential world.

It is true that good Christians were expected in pre-Reformation days to prepare for the fast by confessing their sins and being shriven, a pious custom from which the name of Shrove is derived. But this was only a single aspect of the festival, and probably not the one first thought of when recollecting past Shrovetides or anticipating those to come. The distinguishing mark of the season before Lent was not religious observance but hilarity and feasting and, in greater or lesser degree, it has remained so. After the Reformation, the bell that once called the faithful to be shriven became the Pancake Bell, the signal for sports and games to begin and for pancakes to be made. It is still rung in some parishes on Shrove Tuesday morning, though it no longer has the holiday significance of former times. In England, Shrove Tuesday is called Pancake Day, Guttit Tuesday, or Goodish Day, because of the good things eaten then. In the west-country it is, or was, known as Sharp Tuesday, the day on which local boys claimed an inalienable right to throw stones at people's doors without fear of punishment. In Scotland it is Fasten's E'en, the Eve of the Fast, or Bannock Tuesday, in France and some parts of the United States, Mardi Gras. All these names give us clear little pictures of what the day really meant to countless people in the past, and indeed, what it still means in numerous places where old customs, or some of them, survive and flourish.

Today, except in Carnival-keeping countries, the words "Shrove Tuesday" suggest, first and foremost, pancakes. Although, being dependent on Easter, it is a movable feast, it falls normally in February, or at latest, in the first few days of March. The Roman *Fornacalia,* or Feast of Ovens, fell in February also, and it may be that our pancakes are the direct descendants of the small wheaten cakes eaten then. But if they were pagan in origin, they were Christian in common use, for their making enabled the housewife to dispose of all the remaining fats and butter before the fast began. In the same way, on Collop Monday, bacon, eggs, and fried collops of meat appeared on the table for the last time. Nowadays, there is no longer any need for such wholesale clearances but, though we hear no more of collops, pancakes are still with us and, in innumerable homes, restaurants and hotels, they remain the principal delicacy of Shrove Tuesday.

At Westminster School a pancake is annually scrambled for in the ceremony known as the Pancake Greeze. At eleven o'clock on Shrove Tuesday morning, the cook, preceded by the verger with the silver-topped Mace, enters the Great Schoolroom, carrying a frying pan from which he tosses a pancake over the high bar separating the old Upper and Lower Schools. The assembled boys scramble for the cake as it falls to the ground, and he who secures it, or the largest part of it, receives a guinea from the Dean. The cook is also rewarded for his essential part in the affair. At one time all the boys in the school took part in the scramble, but now each form chooses one of its members to represent it.

Another lively pancake custom, as exclusively feminine as the Westminster Greeze is masculine, is the Pancake Race at Olney in Buckinghamshire. This is said to date from 1445 and to have been carried on, with occasional lapses and revivals, ever since. It consists of a race by the housewives of the township from the square to the church. Each woman carries a frying pan in which she has to toss a pancake three times as she runs. The winner is she who arrives first at the church door with her pancake still intact. She is greeted by the Vicar and kissed by the bell ringer, who is given the cake as his share of the festivity. Thereafter, all the pans are laid at the foot of the font, and competitors, onlookers and clergy take part in a short service of blessing.

Shrovetide is the season for traditional games. In Cornwall there are hurling matches at St. Ives on Quinquagesima Monday, and at St. Columb Major on Shrove Tuesday. Both these were originally street games, played up and down the roads between the houses, and that at St. Columb Major still is. The St. Ives match used to start on the beach, when the Mayor threw a silver-coated ball from the West Pier to the waiting teams below, but in 1939 it was transferred to a public park, thereby losing some of its traditional interest, but not a shred of its popularity and vigor.

At Ashbourne, Atherstone, and some other places, football is played in the open streets between rival parts of a parish or district. Devotees of modern football would scarcely recognize this as the game they know, for there are no obvious rules and in some cases no definite goals, and the size of the teams is regulated only by the number of people who wish to play. It is, in fact, a survival of the rough, wild pastime so often and so fruitlessly forbidden by the authorities in former centuries. At Ashbourne the goals are three miles apart, and between them run the wide Henmore brook and several smaller streams, through which the players have to struggle. At Atherstone the "ground" is the main London-Holyhead road, and all traffic has to be diverted for the occasion. At Alnwick, where the street game has been transferred to a field, the ball is piped there by the Duke of Northumberland's piper; and after the match, there is a fierce struggle to carry the ball over the Duke's boundaries. The first to do so receives a money prize, and certainly he deserves it, for he must not only defeat all his extremely active rivals, but run a breakneck race over hedges, banks, ditches, and at one point, the not inconsiderable River Aln.

Street football also takes place at Corfe Castle in Dorset, but this game is in a slightly different category from the rest, for it serves to maintain an old right of way. Purbeck stone is quarried locally, and on Shrove Tuesday the Ancient Court of Marblers holds its meeting. When that is ended, the quarrymen play a running game of football along the road to Poole, and by so doing preserve the right of carrying stone down it to the harbor from which most of it was formerly shipped.

In Spain, Portugal, Hungary, South Germany, and some other European countries, Shrovetide marks the splendid climax of Carnival, with its many town pageants, its rural revelries, its parades of giants and burnings of effigies, and the inevitable pranks and mischief. Carnival itself is something more than a pre-Lent season of rejoicing in the lands where it is well established. It is a spirit that runs like wildfire through the areas affected, and which is personified in a variety of different figures, real or counterfeit. In the famous celebrations at Nice, it is King Carnival, a monstrous and grotesque giant, who reigns supreme; in northern Spain it is Gregoire, a stuffed figure slightly less fantastic than his colleague in Nice, but still more than life-sized, who rides in an ox-

drawn cart adorned with greenery. In the Rhine-
land there is a human Prince of Carnival, usually
some well-known individual who can afford the
quite heavy expenses connected with his office; and
also there is a human Jester who is the true em-
bodiment of the festival and "dies" when it ends.

This is the season of freedom from ordinary
rules, of noisy fun and masquerades, practical
jokes and ridicule. Mischief is an integral part of
the festivities, as are the organized processions
and dances. In Hungary young men in villages
go round deriding girls whom they consider too
proud, particularly those who have refused suitors
for reasons which their tormentors consider to be
inadequate. They drag round a tree trunk attached
by ropes, and stand outside the culprits' doors,
singing a mocking little song. This can be mere
teasing, and is usually said to be so, but it can
also be spiteful; and so can the custom in some
parts of Switzerland of mocking girls who are still
unmarried beyond the usual age, drenching them
with wine, and driving them out of the Carnival
dances in which their younger companions take
part. In South Germany, the Thursday before Ash
Wednesday is Wives' Night, when women run
through the streets, playing tricks on all the men
they see, and dancing in shops and offices, markets
and railway stations. The days that immediately
follow Wives' Night are called the Three Crazy

Days, when almost anything may happen. Even sober citizens in Carnival-keeping countries sometimes throw shyness to the winds and run about in masks and fancy dress.

But finally the last hour comes, and Carnival must perish. He dies, or is burnt, drowned, or shot, amid the loud ritual wailings of the spectators. The German Jester falls to the ground in the middle of his dancing, and is solemnly carried out on a bier. Gregoire is tried and condemned on Ash Wednesday and burnt upon a pyre, while the people leap and caper around the bonfire and throw flaming brands about. Traditional songs of mourning are sung everywhere, for the merry season is over, and now comes Lent with its privations. "Tomorrow is Ash Wednesday," sing the Hungarians, "Tomorrow it won't be as it is today." That might be reason enough for the ritual laments; but perhaps also, deep down in the subconscious minds of the revelers, there may linger dim memories of the time when the dying Carnival figure was real, the appointed sacrifice to whom the tribute of mourning must be paid, but whose death was necessary to drive the outworn winter and its troubles away, and let the fresh, green spring come in.

Europe is not the only continent which celebrates the age-old festival. Carnival crossed the Atlantic and flowered again in the new soil of

Louisiana, Mississippi, and Alabama. Exactly when it did so is not certain, for more than one southern city claims to be its first American home. There is a pleasant legend that when Pierre Charles d'Iberville planted the French flag in 1699 near the present site of Biloxi, he remembered Shrove Tuesday and feasted his own men and a friendly tribe of Indians with wine, and that this was the first Mardi Gras celebrations ever seen in the New World. Whether he did so or not, Biloxi still holds its annual Carnival in the traditional manner with parades and balls and masquerades. The New Orleans Mardi Gras ceremonies, perhaps the most elaborate and certainly the best-known outside America, were started in 1827 by a group of young men newly returned from France. Those of Mobile began in 1830. The men of the latter city, however, claim that theirs was the first really splendid Mardi Gras, and that New Orleans only burst into its full glory after they had shown the way. Certainly the celebrations in both these and other Southern cities are truly magnificent now; and if perhaps the ancient ritual meaning of the festival is obscured by the fact that Carnival does not die there, but merely goes away, most of the other traditional ceremonies are faithfully kept up, and there is no lack of the genuine gay Carnival spirit anywhere.

3

Mothering Sunday

MID-LENT Sunday, the fourth in Lent, is Mothering Sunday in England, when simnel cakes are eaten, and absent children return home to visit their mothers with gifts of flowers, cakes, and other small things. Before the Reformation it was a cherished festival, the one break in the rigors of Lent, on which games and feasting were permissible, and parishioners in outlying hamlets, who normally worshiped in chapels-of-ease, went to the Mother Church of the parish, there to present their offerings and attend a service. How early the idea of honoring one's own mother on that particular day began is not certain, but clearly it was known in Herrick's time, for he wrote:

I'le to thee a Simnell bring,
'Gainst thou go'st a mothering.
So that, when she blesseth thee,
Half that blessing thou'lt give me.

In 1644 Richard Symonds noted in his *Diary* that "every Mid-Lent Sunday is a great day at Worcester, when all the children and grand-children meet at the head and chief of the family and have a feast. They call it Mothering Day." Throughout the eighteenth and early nineteenth centuries, it was customary for servants and others working away from home to be given a holiday then, so that they might visit their mothers and present them with a cake of their own or their mistress's making, and little posies of violets and other wild flowers gathered in the hedgerows as they walked along the country lanes. The whole family went to church together, and afterwards there was a dinner of roast lamb or veal, at which the mother was treated as queen of the feast, and everything possible was done to make the day memorable for her.

This pleasant custom declined towards the end of the nineteenth century, but of late years it has taken on new life, and has, indeed, become somewhat commercialized, especially in towns where every shop displays advertisements for "Mother's gifts," and the price of flowers soars sharply on the previous Saturday. If families do not go to church together now as often as they did, it is still very usual to see numerous passengers alighting from country buses and trains with bunches of flowers and little parcels in their hands, on their ways to the time-honored family gathering. Many churches hold flower services, to which children bring flowers to be blessed, some to be given to the church and others to their mothers.

In the north of England, the day was once called Braget or Bragot Sunday, because of the spiced ale, or braget, which was the staple drink. Like Shrove Tuesday, though in a lesser degree, it was a day for mischief, a favorite trick of boys being to hook little pieces of colored cloth or paper tails on to the clothes of women going to church. It was also called Simnel Sunday because it was the day for eating simnel cakes.

The ale custom has gone now, and the hooked streamers with it, but simnel cakes are still made and sold in large quantities every year, especially in Lancashire and in the town of Devizes. These cakes are of two main kinds—the Bury simnel, which is a flat spiced cake, thickest in the center, and containing currants, candied peel and almonds, and the better-known Shrewsbury simnel, which is a rich dark cake with a thick, hard crown of almond paste, and garnishings of candied fruits and marzipan flowers. The name simnel is generally supposed to spring from *simila,* the fine wheaten flour of which the cakes are made, but two popular and unreliable legends attempt to explain it otherwise. One says that a man named Simon, and Nell, his wife, quarreled as to whether the mixture should be baked or boiled. They compromised by doing both, and since then the cake has been known by a combination of their two names. The other ascribes it to Lambert Simnel, one of the two false claimants to the throne in Henry VII's reign. According to this tale, his father was a baker, and certain cakes made by him were named after his notorious son. Simnels, however, existed long before his time, for they are mentioned in the *Annals of the Church of Winchester,* where it is stated that in 1042 it was ordered that when the King wore his crown at Winchester, Worcester, or Westminster, the Precentor should receive half a mark from the royal purse, and one hundred simnels and a measure of wine should be given to the convent.

At Bury and Devizes, enormous numbers of simnels are made every year and sent all over the world. In both towns baking begins soon after Christmas, so as to allow time for the cakes to reach people abroad by Mothering Sunday. In some cases, standing orders left by men who emigrated to America or the Dominions nearly a century ago are still being fulfilled, the orders having been renewed by their children and grandchildren after the deaths of the original emigrants.

At Chilbolton in Hampshire, Mid-Lent wafers take the place of simnels on Mothering Sunday. The recipe is a secret one, handed down from mother to daughter in one family for several generations. With the increasing age of the last member of that family, some doubt has arisen as to the future of this centuries-old custom, which may disappear unless the secret can be transferred to someone else. The wafers are cooked by pouring batter on to the bottom plate of a pair of wafering irons made very hot in a wood fire, and pressing it down with the other to form crisp and fragile wafers printed with ecclesiastical symbols and, on one side, the letters I S. The irons themselves are known to be three hundred years old, and when not in use, they are kept in the Winchester Museum for safety. When these Mid-Lent wafers were first made is not known, but almost certainly it was in pre-Reformation times. One local tradition says that in the Middle Ages they were manufactured in a nearby monastery, and were distributed to the faithful when they visited the Mother Church on Mid-Lent Sunday.

In Scotland formerly, the family gatherings were not held on Mothering Sunday, but on

Passion or Carling Sunday, the fifth in Lent. Car-cakes, a species of highly flavored pancake, were the children's traditional gift, and carlings, or gray peas soaked in water and fried in butter, were eaten at the feast. This dish also appeared on English tables on Passion Sunday, which is still called Carling or Care Sunday in some parts of the north. The origin of the name is obscure, but by many it is supposed to refer to the sufferings, or care, of Our Lord's Passion, which now begins to be foreshadowed in the ceremonies of the Church.

Since World War II there has been a tendency in many parts of England to refer to Mothering Sunday as Mother's Day. This is due to the influence of American soldiers stationed in Britain during that war, though the transatlantic anniversary to which the name really belongs has nothing to do with Mid-Lent Sunday, and falls in May, not during Lent. Perhaps because of the strong Protestant traditions of the early settlers, Mothering Sunday did not cross the ocean as some of the other folk festivals did. In 1907 it occurred to Miss Anna Jarvis, of Philadelphia, that there should be one day in the year when children specially honored their mothers. She arranged for a special service to be held in one of the local churches, and asked those who attended it to wear white carnations. The success of this first effort inspired her to work for its nation-wide observance, and within a few years, the new anniversay had spread all over the United States and into Canada and several Latin-American countries. In 1914 Congress crowned her work by fixing the second Sunday in May as Mother's Day throughout the States. The presentation of gifts and the wearing of carnations—white in memory of mothers already dead and red to honor those still living—has now become an established American custom on Mother's Day. Although this festival is quite new and, unlike Mothering Sunday, is not rooted in any ancient religious tradition, it has taken a strong hold on the hearts of the people, and by now, in spite of its organized and official character, it may be said to rank as a true folk custom likely to persist for many generations to come.

4

Palms and Gifts

ON Palm Sunday Holy Week begins, the time of the Passion of Our Lord which ended in the darkness on Calvary. From then onwards, the shadows deepen in all the Church's rites, and devout Christians observe the four following days as a period of mourning and penitence. Nevertheless, Palm Sunday itself is traditionally a day of rejoicing, for it is the anniversary of Christ's triumphal entry into Jerusalem, when the people shouted for joy all round Him, spreading their garments before the feet of the humble ass He rode, and tearing down branches from the trees to throw in its path. The memory of that event has been honored from early times by the carrying of blessed palms in procession, and the distribution of small sprigs or palm crosses to congregations in the churches. This custom has never ceased in Roman Catholic countries, though some of the more elaborate details of the processions have disappeared; but after the Reformation, it declined in Protestant lands, where it was often regarded as a mere relic of "popery." Yet the association of palms or willows with this Sunday of early spring never quite faded from popular tradition anywhere, and of late years their use in decorations and their distribution to worshipers have been revived in many churches and chapels from which such rites were formely excluded.

In England, the Sallow Willow, with its large and beautiful catkins, often takes the place of the true palm, which does not grow there and has to be imported from Spain. Where willows are scarce, box or hazel is pressed into service and used, like the willow, to decorate houses as well as churches. At one time, men and boys regularly went "a-palming" in the three or four days beforehand, gathering great branches of greenery and fluffy, golden catkins to adorn their homes, and sprigs to wear in their hats. If they did not always connect these expeditions with the religious festival, they were certain it was the right thing to do at that season, because it had always been done, and that the "palms" so gathered brought good luck and protected the houses that contained them from evil.

The Welsh name for the feast is *Sul y Blodau,* or Flowering Sunday, the day on which the family graves in the churchyard are strewn with flowers. In some parts of the Principality the name is applied to Easter Sunday instead, and in those areas the dressing of the graves is deferred to the later date. In both cases a ritual preparation for Easter seems to be indicated, the dead sharing with the living in the Resurrection symbolism of the new-sprung flowers. Another pleasant custom, still found in many Welsh parishes, which may have some connection with the grave-strewing rite, is that of presenting friends and neighbors with small posies of spring blossoms on Easter morning.

Older people sometimes refer to Palm Sunday as Fig Sunday, though the custom from which the name springs has died out now almost entirely. Until comparatively recently, however, it was usual to eat figs, or fig pudding, at the midday dinner, and enormous quantities of the fruit were annually sold for the purpose. Children were given little packets of figs also, and told to remember the Parable of the Barren Fig Tree while they ate them. Little more than ninety years ago, people in some parts of Hertfordshire and Wiltshire used to gather on some local hill on Palm Sunday, there to make merry, eat figs, and drink each other's healths in ale or cider; but this cheerful custom, like the eating of fig puddings at home, is forgotten now.

Another English name for the festival is Spanish Sunday. This rather unexpected title comes from the children's habit of making a sweetish drink from broken pieces of Spanish liquorice shaken up in a bottle of water. No ordinary water from a tap may be used on this occasion. It has to be drawn from some particular holy or wishing well in the neighborhood, and a special pilgrimage must be made to fetch it. At one period, not so long ago, such wells were visited by crowds of children from all the nearby parishes, and even in these sophisticated days, little groups can often be seen, solemnly walking three times round the well, filling and shaking their bottles, and happily drinking the resulting concoction. This odd little ceremony has no obvious connection with the Christian Palm Sunday, and one variant of the rite suggests that it may be a fragmentary relic of ancient well worship. In some Derbyshire villages formerly, the children went to the well on Palm Sunday and dropped new pins therein. On Easter Monday they returned and filled their bottles in the usual manner. They said that if they omitted to offer the pins first, the "Lady of the Well" would not let them have clean water, and their "Easter Monday bottles" would break.

A ceremony intended to preserve peace between neighbors and reconcile the estranged is annually held on Palm Sunday at Hentland in Hereford-shire. As the congregation comes out of church after the morning service, each member receives from the clergyman a small cake, called a Pax Cake, and is greeted by him with the words "God and Good Neighbourhood." It is not known how old this custom is, for no documentary evidence of its foundation survives. Local tradition says, however, that in the sixteenth century Lady Scudamore, a landowner in the district, left money to provide for the distribution of cake and beer to all the parishioners of Hentland, Sellack, and King's Caple. She did this because she thought that those who had thus shared a common feast on Palm Sunday would be more likely to compose their differences and be at peace with one another, and that so, they would be able to make their Easter Communion more worthily. In spite of this tradition, the ceremony may well be older than the sixteenth century. It has a pre-Reformation flavor about it, especially in its original and un-altered form, and it is possible that, as in some other cases of customs supported by the bequests of benefactors, Lady Scudamore's money may have

been left in 1570 to preserve a rite already exist-
ing in her time, rather than to institute a new
one.

In the course of centuries, the custom has
changed slightly, though the underlying idea remains the same. Originally the food and drink
were consumed in the church itself. One large
cake was provided, the first slice being cut by the
priest, and the rest carried round by the church-
wardens to the people in their seats. Glasses of
beer were also given until about the middle of the
nineteenth century. The funds needed to pay for
them seem to have been lost then, perhaps owing
to the fall in the value of money; and although
it is said that some conservatively minded individuals tried to supply the lack by bringing
their own home-brewed beer or cider to the service, changing ideas of what was fitting probably
prevented any serious attempt to restore this
part of the ceremony after it had once lapsed.
Later on, small cakes stamped with the figure of
the Lamb and Flag were substituted for the single
large one, and these are now no longer eaten in
the church, but are presented to each person as he
or she leaves the building.

Maundy Thursday is said to derive its English
name from *mandatum*, a command, in reference
to the new commandment of love which Our Lord
gave to His Apostles at the Last Supper. This was

also the day on which maunds, or gifts, were given to the poor after the ceremony of Washing the Feet, once annually performed in most Christian countries. Another old name was Chare, or Shere Thursday, which probably refers to the ceremonial cleansing of altars in churches, and perhaps also to the cleaning of houses in preparation for Easter.

From a very early period in the Church's history, it was customary for priests and others to wash the feet of twelve or more poor people, in memory of the supreme example of humility set by Christ on the night before His death. In later times, gifts of money, food, and clothes were added, and the originally simple ceremony gradually became a solemn and splendid function in which kings and high dignitaries of the Church took part. In Rome today, the Pope washes the feet of thirteen priests and serves them at table with bread and wine. Of the thirteen, twelve represent the Apostles, and the other who, unlike the rest, is always a young man, represents the Angel who is traditionally said to have come to the table when St. Gregory the Great was serving it. Before the Russian Revolution, a like ceremony was conducted by the Archbishop in Moscow, and in Austria the Emperor, attended by the Archdukes of the Blood Royal, first washed the feet of twelve old men, and then feasted them at a splendid dinner of many courses. Similar rites took place at one time in Spain and also in France.

In England, the Maundy custom seems to have been known at least as early as the seventh century, when it was mainly in the hands of monks. During the Middle Ages, kings and sometimes great nobles also, distributed gifts and washed the feet, not of twelve people only, but of as many as there were years in their own age. We are told that Edward III, when he was fifty years old, ministered thus to fifty poor men, and afterwards gave them each a pair of slippers. At one period the Sovereign gave the gown he was wearing, but later this was redeemed by a money payment. In the reign of Elizabeth I, the redemption fee paid to each person was twenty shillings, a fairly considerable sum in those days, and this amount is still given, with other monies, at the modern Maundy distributions.

The last English king to perform the full rite was James II, who, according to a record kept at Somerset House, "on Maundy Thursday, April 16th 1685 . . . wash'd, wip'd and kiss'd the feet of 52 poor men with wonderful humility." After his time, this part of the ceremony was omitted, and until 1932, the presentation of the Maundy gifts was made by proxy, the Lord High Almoner taking the place of the sovereign. In that year, however, George V "made his Maunds" in person, the first English king to do so since James II, and each of his successors, including the present Queen, has done the same on various occasions.

In earlier centuries, the gifts were of several sorts, including woolen and linen cloth for garments, shoes, stockings, food and money. In 1572 Queen Elizabeth gave thirty-nine poor women a length of broadcloth, a pair of sleeves, salmon on a wooden platter, ling, six red herrings, six loaves, claret, the aprons worn by her attendants, and the towels she had used for the feet washing. Now money is given in lieu of the food and cloth, with an additional twenty shillings for the redemption of the royal gown, and specially minted Maundy coins corresponding in number with the age of the giver. These last are current coin of the realm and could be spent like the rest; but usually they are treasured as mementoes of a splendid occasion, and so rarely pass into general circulation.

The Maundy ceremony normally takes place in Westminster Abbey, but it can be held elsewhere, and in 1959, Queen Elizabeth II presented her gifts at St. Albans. The lovely and colorful rite begins with the processional entry of the officiating clergy, carrying little posies of flowers and having linen towels girt round them in memory of the lost custom of washing the feet. Choirboys in their scarlet cassocks and canons in their ceremonial copes precede them, and behind them come the Children of the Royal Almonry, also bearing flowers and towels, wandsmen, other clergy, and the Yeoman of the Guard, two of whom carry the dishes on which the leather purses are piled, their long red or white thongs hanging over the edges like a fringe. There is a service that includes prayers, hymns and anthems, and then the Queen, if she is present, and if she is not, the Lord High Almoner, now in simple white, his splendid vestments doffed, passes down the waiting lines of old people, one man and one woman for each year of the Queen's age, presents the purses, and bows to the recipients. (In 1960 Queen Elizabeth the Queen Mother distributed the Royal Maundy on behalf of the Queen.)

The purses are of various colors—red for the money paid to redeem the gown, white for the men's allowance in lieu of clothes, green for the women's allowance, and white with red thongs for the Maundy coins. There are two distributions, the first for the white, green and red purses, and the second for the red and white, with their silver pennies, twopenny, threepenny and fourpenny pieces specially made for the occasion. When all is done, the officiants return to their places, and the impressive ceremony ends with further prayers, the Blessing, and the singing of the national anthem by everyone in the church.

5

Good Friday

FROM very early times, Good Friday has been observed by Christians everywhere as the most solemn feast of the year, a day of penitence and mourning, when the Passion and Death of Our Lord is remembered in countless churches by services of sorrow and gratitude. Its various names, both those still in use and those that have become obsolete, all stress its supreme religious importance. In English-speaking countries it is Good Friday, which is usually thought to be a corruption of God's Friday. Elsewhere in Europe it is often Holy or Great Friday, and in Denmark it is *Langfredag*, or Long Friday, the word "long" in this case having much the same meaning as "great." In Anglo-Saxon England it was Long Friday also, and at Brighton, in Sussex, a variant of the old title survived until about the middle of last century in the form of Long Rope Day. This indicated not only the festival itself, using its ancient name, but also an odd custom observed by the fishing community. Men, women, and children went down to the beach and there skipped vigorously with ropes from the boats. In the course of time, adults ceased to take part in this pastime, and gradually, like so many old customs, it fell entirely into the hands of the children, and finally died out altogether. In northern England, the day was sometimes called Care Friday because, like Care (or Passion) Sunday and Care (or Holy) Week before it, it was a time of sorrow.

Good Friday is now an official holiday in numerous countries, including Great Britain and some parts of the United States, and for many it has come to mean chiefly an escape from shops and factories into the bright springtime world. Yet even among the least devout there is often a deep-rooted feeling that this is a day apart from all others. One very common manifestation of this feeling was, and still is in some instances, a reluctance to do customary work then, either from genuine respect for the religious festival, or from superstitious fears that to do it will somehow bring misfortune.

Until very recently, miners refused to go down the pit on Good Friday, believing that some disaster in the mine would follow if they did. Blacksmiths also, in the heyday of their trade, would not shoe a horse, or work in any other way with nails, because of the dreadful use to which nails had once been put on Calvary. In the Isle of Man, householders never used iron tools in the home then for much the same reason. Fire irons and griddles were all put away beforehand, and if the fire needed poking, it was done with a rowan-wood stick instead of the poker. Farmers did not work with horses, and along the coasts, fishermen stayed ashore, considering it both impious and ill-omened to put to sea on that day.

A very widespread belief, by no means extinct yet, was that it is extremely unlucky to wash clothes or linen on Good Friday. Legend says that whoever does so will find the water stained with blood, or the clothes hung on the line spotted with it, and that misfortune of some kind, perhaps a death in the family, will follow. Probably no one believes that now, but a vague tradition of ill luck still clings about Good Friday washing, and older housewives usually avoid doing it themselves, and are faintly shocked if they hear of any one else doing it. On the other hand, their husbands, if they are keen gardeners, choose that day for planting potatoes and parsley, as in Spain they choose it for setting melons and marrows. Country tradition says that seeds put in the earth then will always thrive, because on that one day of the year the soil is redeemed from the power of Satan.

At Ayot St. Peter in Hertfordshire, they ring the Nine Tailors for Our Lord's death, as in many other parishes they ring them for the deaths of ordinary men. Ringing the Nine Tailors (or tellers) is an ancient method of notifying the living that someone in the district has died. The bell is tolled nine times for a man, six for a woman, and three for a child, and then, after a short pause, it is tolled again to indicate the dead person's age. So at Ayot St. Peter on Good Friday, it rings nine times for the Man Who died then, followed by thirty-three strokes for His age.

Eating hot cross buns is one of the few Good Friday customs that has taken root in America. Piping hot from the oven, they appear on innumerable breakfast tables on both sides of the Atlantic Ocean, pleasantly spiced, and with their shiny brown tops marked by a deeply cut cross. Most people believe that this cross is a purely Christian emblem, connected with the day on which the cakes are traditionally eaten. It may, however, be far older. The cross was a pagan symbol long before it acquired everlasting significance from the events of the first Good Friday, and bread and cakes were sometimes marked with it in pre-Christian times. Two small loaves, each with a cross on it, were discovered under the ruins of Herculaneum, the city that was overwhelmed by volcanic ash in A.D. 79. It is, of course, just possible that they were made for some isolated Christian citizen, but it is not very likely; it is far more probable that the crosses here had a pagan meaning, like those which appeared on cakes associated with the worship of Diana. If, as seems possible, the little wheaten cakes that are known to have been made at primitive Spring Festivals were similarly marked, our hot cross buns can claim a long and deeply interesting lineage, running back into very remote times.

However that may be, they are now a distinctive feature of our Good Friday customs, and have been so for a long time. Once they were made at home by housewives who rose at dawn to have them ready for the family breakfast, or by bakers working through the night, so that the street vendors could be out in good time with their laden trays and their cries of "Hot Cross Buns! One a penny, two a penny, Hot Cross Buns!" But now that bakers no longer work at night, and housewives only rarely bake their own bread and buns, the little cakes are usually made and delivered on the previous day, and simply heated up again for breakfast.

It is not always realized that this fact deprives them of most of their traditional virtues, or should do so, according to old belief. Not so long ago, it was believed that those baked on the holy day itself, and also bread made then, had curative and magical properties. They never went moldly. If hardened in the oven, they could be kept all the year, and their presence in the house protected it from fire. Sailors took them on their voyages to prevent shipwreck; in Florida, as late as 1879, three Good Friday loaves thrust into a heap of corn were considered sufficient to protect it from the ravages of rats, mice, and weevils. The commonest use of such bread or buns was as a cure for diarrhea, dysentery and kindred complaints. They were finely grated, mixed with milk or water, and given to the patient as a medicine. This has been done within living memory, and indeed, faith in the old remedy is not quite dead even yet. But those who believed most sincerely insisted that only the loaves or buns actually made on Good Friday were efficacious, for it was the sanctity of the festival itself which endowed them with their curative powers.

Two interesting customs connected with hot cross buns are annually kept up in London. One takes place at an inn called The Widow's Son, where a bun is ceremonially laid in a basket containing many others by a sailor who receives free beer as his reward. In the early nineteenth century, the licensee of this inn was a widow. Her son was a sailor, and every year, if he happened to be at sea on Good Friday, she laid aside a hot cross bun against the day of his return. One year, however, he did not return, nor did he ever do so again. She would not give up hope, and continued to keep a bun for him, hanging it up in the bar parlor until the next Good Friday came round, and then laying it in the basket with its predecessors. After her death, later tenants did the same, and now a clause in the lease enforces the custom. During World War II the collection was housed in a skittle alley under the bar to ensure its safety during air raids. Many of the older buns are still in a state of perfect preservation, but some of those made with inferior flour during the two wars are already crumbling away.

In the other London custom, the hot cross bun is only incidental, but it is never omitted. Every Good Friday, twenty-one poor widows come to a certain tombstone in the churchyard of St. Bartholomew-the-Great in Smithfield. Each one picks up a sixpence laid upon it by the church-wardens, walks over the stone, and then receives a hot cross bun and a further half-crown. Who first instituted this benefaction is now unknown, for the relevant documents were lost with the other parish records in the Great Fire of 1666. The charity itself, with its curious insistence on stepping over the grave, might have been lost too, for the funds were long since diverted to another purpose. Other monies were, however, provided by the generosity of a London antiquary, and so the widows still receive their dole of three shillings and their hot cross bun.

In Portugal, countryfolk and sailors burn a straw or wood effigy of Judas Iscariot on Good Friday. The figure is beaten, kicked, cursed and derided, and finally it is either burnt or hanged, amid the jeers of the crowds who gather to watch. Elsewhere, too, Judas is punished in various ways, both in Europe and in some South American countries, to which the custom traveled with the Portuguese and Spanish colonists. In Corfu, crockery is violently hurled down a steep hill, each person calling down curses on the traitor as he throws it. In Devonshire, as late as the end of last century, crockery was regularly broken on Good Friday in the belief that the jagged edges of each broken piece would pierce the body of the betrayer. At one time, a straw figure called Jack-a-Lent was dragged about on Ash Wednesday in many English parishes, pelted with stones and mud, and then burnt or shot to pieces with guns. It was supposed to represent Judas Iscariot, and probably it did in most people's minds; but its name, and the fact that in the seventeenth century it seems to have been destroyed, not on Ash Wednesday as in later times, but on Palm Sunday, suggests that it may also have symbolized the Lenten fast, like Prince Cibere in Hungary. "Then Jake à Lent comes justlynge in . . ." wrote Elderton in the ballad called *Lenton Stuff,*

> And to Palme Sonday doethe he ryde,
> With sports and herrynges by hys syde,
> And makes an end of Lenton tyde.

Liverpool children still "burn Judas" at Easter in some parts of the city. Very early in the morning, bands of girls and boys, all with blackened faces, may be seen marching through the streets, carrying with them a roughly made figure of a man dressed in whatever old clothes they have been able to beg or steal. Parents have to watch their possessions closely as the time draws near, for new garments are quite as likely to be taken, if opportunity offers, as old ones. Only a few years ago, one father found his best suit had been commandeered for the purpose. The children parade through the district, shouting "Judas! Judas!" until they weary of the game. Then they make a bonfire in a side street, or on some convenient waste ground or bomb site, throw the effigy into the flames, and dance wildly round it with joined hands, shouting in triumph as it burns.

On Good Friday, the last of the great *Semana Santa* processions winds its way in the chill of the early morning through the streets of Spanish towns. These elaborate and impressive parades begin in some places on Palm Sunday, when every window and balcony is decked with palms, and continue nightly until Good Friday. Tableaux depicting the events of the first Holy Week, and splendid images of Our Lord, the Madonna, and the Saints, their robes encrusted with jewels that flash in the light of hundreds of candles, are carried on huge platforms along routes thickly lined with spectators. With them go the *Nazarenos,* the penitents, walking bare footed, their heads completely covered by pointed black or white hoods in which eye holes have been cut to enable their wearers to see. Drums beat monotonously as the long procession moves forward; trumpets sound their high, clear notes, and in Granada, the great bell of the Cathedral tolls continuously. Towards the end of the parade, melancholy and beautiful *saetas* are sung, plaintive songs lamenting the death of Christ and the grief of His mother. The watching crowds weep and pray, and there is a genuine sense of mourning everywhere. But there is also gaiety and excitement, a joyous feeling running under and through the sorrow, for this is springtime, and beyond the shadows of Good Friday lie the end of Lent and fasting, and the coming glories of Easter.

The most famous of these religious processions are those of Seville, Granada, and Malaga, but there are others like them in many parts of Spain, Portugal, the Basque country, and Sicily. In the high valleys of the Pyrenees, the villagers themselves sometimes act the part of those concerned in the Good Friday story. A young man carries a heavy wooden cross, his back bent beneath its weight as he toils along the rough roads. Beside and behind him come women representing the Virgin Mary and Mary Cleophas, St. Veronica with her miraculously marked veil, and Mary Magdalen. Roman soldiers walk or ride in the parades, with dark-robed Penitents, and children bearing emblems of the Passion. Here too, the drums beat, their sinister note heightened in some places by the rhythmic thudding of the Roman soldiers' spears. At Hijar, young men in masks and black robes go about singly with drums which they beat without ceasing for three days and nights. The maddening, unrelenting noise sends everyone almost distracted, but it is willingly endured because in popular belief it drives away the Devil and his evil hosts.

6

Easter Day

AT Easter all things are renewed for the festival of the Resurrection. The churches that were left bare, dark, and empty on Good Friday are filled with flowers and greenery, and lit at every service by the great Paschal Candle that burns from then onwards to Ascension Day. Every kind of spring flower can be used in the decorations—primroses, daffodils, narcissi, anemones, jonquils, and branches from the many trees in blossom at this season—but chief among them all is the arum lily which of late years has come to be regarded as the supreme Easter flower. Colored flowers of many hues adorn the nave, the side chapels, and the transepts, where these exist; but on the altar itself there is usually only white and green, the pure white of the lilies, and the dark green of the yew branches which signify immortality.

In the Roman Catholic and Orthodox communions, and in some High Anglican churches, new fire is kindled at midnight on Easter Eve by the ancient method of striking flint against steel. At the beginning of the service, the church is all in darkness, in memory of the time when Christ lay in the tomb and the Light of the World was hidden from men's sight. The congregation waits in silence, seeing nothing but what seems like the movement of shadows as the priests and servers pass down the nave. Then the small sound of steel scraping upon flint is heard. A minute flame pierces the darkness and is caught upon a piece of charcoal. This is the "new fire," the spark obtained by friction, which from remote pagan times has symbolized regeneration and holiness, and now symbolizes the Resurrection. It is solemnly blessed, and from it the Paschal Candle, and later the other candles, are lit. At this service also, the water that will be used in Baptism is blessed in a most beautiful form of words. In some countries, after the baptismal water has been thus sanctified, the priest goes out of the church and blesses all the wells, cisterns, pools, and running streams of the district.

It is customary almost everywhere to put on

new clothes at Easter, a whole outfit if possible, but if not, then at least a new hat, or a new pair of gloves. Not so long ago, young men often sent gloves to the girls of their choice on Easter Eve. If these were accepted and worn next day at the morning service, it was a sign that the courtship was going well, and was likely to end in marriage. Country people say that if any one is so indifferent as to wear only old clothes to the Sunday service, the crows will befoul his or her garments, and bad luck of a more serious kind will follow. Poverty cannot be offered as an excuse, for if nothing more can be afforded, a new tie or scarf, some ribbons, or even a pair of shoelaces is enough. It need hardly be said, however, that this superstition is much younger than the custom it seems to enforce. Long before Christianity came to the world, people put on fresh, new garments at the Spring Festival, for joy that the winter was past; and since, even in this artificial age, few are so dull of heart as to be quite unaffected by that recurrent happiness, it is probable that they will go on doing so for a long time to come.

Houses, too, are "cleaned down" in readiness for Easter. In an early sixteenth-century book called *The Festival* we are told how:

This daye is called in many places, Godde's Sondaye; ye know well that it is the maner at this daye to do the fyre out of the hall, and the blacke winter brandes, and all thynges that is foule with fume and smoke shall be done awaye, and there the fyre was shall be gayly arrayed with fayre floures, and strewed with grene rysshes al aboute.

That was written before the calendar reform of 1752 made every English anniversary eleven days earlier than it had been previously, and so, as far as early spring dates are concerned, likely to be eleven days colder. The modern Easter is not always warm enough to "do the fyre out of the hall," and serious spring cleaning has usually to be deferred until later in the year. Nevertheless, housewives still clean their rooms against the festival and brighten them with flowers, and in some homes the traditional foods are prepared—roast lamb and mint sauce, or veal, custard tarts sprinkled with currants, and the flat, round, rather thick biscuits known as Easter Cakes. Puddings flavored with tansy juice were formely eaten with the meat course. They were supposed to commemorate the herbs eaten at the Passover meal, and for that reason they were rarely omitted; but they are too bitter for modern taste, and today they are hardly ever seen.

Easter eggs appear on most family breakfast tables, either the true dyed eggs of tradition or its chocolate substitute, or perhaps both together. Sometimes there are little be-ribboned parcels by each person's plate. The habit of giving small presents to near relatives, as well as eggs, is now far commoner than it was fifty or sixty years ago. Recently too, Easter cards, with religious designs, or pictures of flowers, lambs, eggs, or the Easter Hare, have become very popular as tokens of remembrance between friends.

In Sweden children in odd disguises go round on Easter Eve with a special kind of greeting. This is the *Pask brev,* or Easter letter, which nowadays takes the form of a folded paper adorned with drawings and the words *Glad Pask* (happy Easter). The most usual subject is a witch flying on a broomstick. This is because the witches of Sweden are traditionally supposed to fly to Blackula or some other meeting place at Easter, there to hold conference with the Devil. Once the letter contained verses used by the witches themselves on these occasions, but now simple drawings are more usual. The children push them through the letter boxes in their friends' houses, and then they let off crackers and fireworks in the street. The latter custom is a relic from the days when their elders lit bonfires or fired guns to drive away the flying witches from their houses.

In Russia, Poland, and other Eastern European countries, the traditional greeting on Easter Day is

"Christ is Risen!" to which the person greeted replies, "He is risen indeed." Three kisses are then exchanged, always if the people concerned know each other well, and quite often even when they do not. The Easter Table is set out in almost every house and spread with the richest food the family can afford. This is eaten at any time from early morning onwards, with no fixed hour or order. It is blessed beforehand by the priest, either in the home or in church. Where the parish is small, the priest comes in person to pronounce a blessing over it and sprinkle it with holy water; but if his district is too large to allow him to visit every house, the children of the family take samples of everything that will be eaten to the church on Easter Eve, so that he may bless it there.

In Poland, the table itself is decorated with green leaves. In the center stands a lamb made of sugar, bearing the sacred flag, and all round it, on the best china dishes available, are cold roast pork, ham, sausages, salads of various kinds, cakes and sweetmeats, and every sort of regional delicacy. There may also be small models of the main foods made of colored marzipan. Easter eggs, called *pisanki,* are always included. These, like their counterparts elsewhere, are hard-boiled, dyed or painted in bright colors, and sometimes decorated with elaborate designs. Various legends are told to account for their presence on the Easter

Table. One is that when Mary Magdalen and her companions went to the Sepulchre with sweet spices to annoint Our Lord's body, they also took a few eggs in a basket to eat when their work was done. On their arrival at the tomb, they found that these had miraculously taken on all colors of the rainbow. Another charming tale relates how the first *pisanki* were made by Our Lady herself in the peaceful days at Nazareth, long before the shadows of Calvary fell across her life. To amuse the Infant Jesus, she took eggs from her household store, boiled them hard, and painted them red and green and yellow. Since then, say the Polish countrywomen, every good mother or housewife has done the same, but because eggs are symbols of new life, they do it now on the Resurrection festival.

A very old belief, once found in most parts of Great Britain and Ireland, was that the sun danced at its rising on Easter morning, for joy that Our Lord had risen from the grave. Those who were up early enough could sometimes see it doing so, especially if they climbed to the top of a hill where nothing could obstruct their view of so lovely a sight. As late as the middle of last century, people went in large numbers to hilltops and open spaces, and watched to see the sun leap and change color or, as some said, swing round and round like a wheel. Many declared they did see it, and probably they did, perhaps through faith alone, or perhaps because of the flickering effect sometimes visible in a sunrise viewed from a high place. One old Highland woman told the author of *Carmina Gaedelica* that she had seen the miracle only once in her life, and had never forgotten it. "The glorious gold-bright sun was after rising on the crests of the great hills," she said, "and it was changing colour—green, purple, red, blood-red, white, intense-white, and gold-white, like the glory of the God of the elements to the children of men. It was dancing up and down in exultation at the joyous resurrection of the beloved Saviour of victory."

A kindred belief, less widespread than the dancing tradition but very firmly held in some districts, was that the image of the Lamb and Flag—the Lamb carrying the red cross banner—appeared in the center of the sun's disk on Easter morning. It was visible only in the first few moments after the sun had risen, and country people used to get up early to go and look at it. Some took pieces of smoked glass with them, but many declared that they had seen the image, clearly and distinctly, with their unprotected eyes. Until comparatively recently, a form of sunrise divination was practiced on the same day in the fenland regions of Lincolnshire. A bucket of water was set down in some open space where the first rays of the rising sun would fall upon it. If the light shone steadily and clearly in the water, it was a sign that the coming season would bring fine weather and a good harvest, but if the reflection was tremulous and uncertain, it foretold poor crops and a cold, wet summer.

Easter Eve bonfires are still lit in Holland, Germany and southern Sweden, as they once were in many European countries, including England. In some rural districts of Holland, the boys chase the girls round the fires and throw soot all over them. This lively and messy practice is not resented by the victims because it is supposed to bring good luck. In fact, it is a direct survival of an ancient fertility rite, but probably few of the onlookers, or the young people most nearly concerned, remember that now. At Fredericksburg in Texas, the same age-old fires blaze on Holy Saturday on the tops of nearby hills. The custom was brought there by Germans who settled in the district about the middle of last century, and it has continued ever since. Hundreds go every year to see the huge bonfires lit; fireworks are let off or thrown into the flames, the bells ring in the churches, and who knows how many of those present cherish at least a half-belief that the ritual may really bring them luck, as it did to their far-off European ancestors? The explanation of all this pagan merriment, which is given to the local children, is that the Easter Rabbit is burning wild flowers to make dyes for the Easter eggs.

There is a well-known English saying which runs,

If Our Lord falls in Our Lady's lap,
England will meet with a great mishap.

or in other words, if Easter (or according to some, Good Friday) falls on March 25th, which is Lady Day, some national misfortune will follow before the next Eastertide comes round. The origin of this is an old but unsubstantiated tradition that the Crucifixion took place on March 25th, and the consequent belief that it is ill-omened for the Day of Resurrection to fall then, or for Good Friday to coincide with its supposed original date. It may be of interest to note that, twice in this century, the ancient prophecy seems to have been fulfilled. In 1910 Good Friday was on March 25th, and in the following May, Edward VII died after a short illness. In 1951, Easter Sunday fell on the same ominous date, and on February 6th, not quite eleven months afterwards, that deeply loved king, George VI, died peacefully but very suddenly at Sandringham.

7

Easter Eggs

EASTER eggs have a very long ancestry. In their modern chocolate or cardboard form, they date only from the later years of last century, but the giving of real eggs, colored or gilded, at Easter, and also at the pre-Christian Spring Celebrations, is infinitely older. Long before the Christian era, eggs were regarded as symbols of continuing life and resurrection. The ancient Persians, Greeks and Chinese exchanged them at their Spring Festivals, when all things in Nature revived after the winter; and in several pagan mythologies we hear of the World Egg, from which the divine Sun-Bird was hatched, or from

61

the two halves of which Heaven and Earth were formed. To the early Christians, eggs seemed obvious symbols of Our Lord's Resurrection, and they were therefore considered holy and appropriate gifts at Eastertide. In pre-Reformation times they were blessed and used in the Easter ceremonies at the church. "Bless, O Lord, we beseech Thee," says a prayer appointed by Pope Paul V for use in England, Scotland and Ireland, "this Thy creature of eggs, that it may become a wholesome sustenance to Thy faithful servants, eating in thankfulness to Thee, on account of the Resurrection of Our Lord." During the long fast of Lent they were forbidden food, but on Easter Day they were joyfully eaten once more, and given as presents to friends, servants, and all the members of the family.

The custom of coloring eggs at Easter may well be as old as the festival itself, continuing with only a change of dedication from the earlier pagan usage. Certainly it was known in England during the Middle Ages, for in Edward I's household accounts for 1290, there is an entry of eighteenpence spent on the purchase of four hundred and fifty eggs which were to be colored, or covered with leaf gold, for distribution to the Royal Household. In many English homes today, the dyed and decorated hen's or duck's egg still appears on the Easter breakfast table, side by side with its chocolate or marzipan descendant. It can be of any color, but quite often it is red. Tradition says this commemorates the blood of Christ, shed for us on Good Friday; but scarlet eggs were given in spring by the Chinese and other pagan peoples centuries before the birth of Our Lord, and probably this favorite color was chosen originally because, like the egg itself, it is an emblem of life.

The old method of tinting eggs was to boil them with flowers or leaves, logwood chips, or cochineal. Spinach leaves or anemone petals could be used for greens, gorse blossom for yellow, logwood for a rich purple, and cochineal for scarlet. Nowadays, vegetable or aniline dyes provide a variety of gay colors—blue, green, primrose, brown, purple, orange, rose, or vivid red. An egg boiled with the outer skin of an onion wrapped round it comes out a delicately mottled yellow, or a variegated effect can be obtained by binding it with strips of colored rag or ribbon. In Switzerland, minute flowers and leaves are bound on before boiling in onion peel, to produce a white pattern on the tinted ground. Sometimes a design, a message, or the name of the recipient is traced on the already dyed egg with a white wax pencil, or the color is carefully scratched off with a sharp knife, leaving white lines or letters behind.

In Eastern Europe, painting Easter eggs is a traditional peasant art. Often they are red, but in

Hungary they are more usually white, with a red flower pattern drawn upon them. The design is first traced on with wax, and then the eggs are dipped into cold paint. Sometimes they are shod with tiny metal shoes, complete with spurs, and have small metal hangers attached to them. Hungarian children exchange painted eggs as tokens of friendship, and in some parts of the country, they are hung, with other things, on the little Easter trees which young men set up outside the houses of the girls they admire.

In Yugoslavia, they are always marked with the letters X V, for *Christos vaskrese* (Christ is risen), the traditional Easter greeting of Eastern Europe. In Poland, geometrical or abstract patterns are often used, or Christian symbols like the Fish and the Cross. Formerly, Polish girls gave their favored suitors anything from thirty to a hundred eggs, which they either decorated themselves, if they were sufficiently skillful, or sent to one of the women who specialized in the art. Before the first World War, such specialists existed in most villages. Each one knew a great number of intricate designs, and a few were renowned for their artistry far beyond the confines of their own parish. Their work was rewarded by money or goods or, if the client lacked the means to pay otherwise, by help given in the house. When the decorating was finished, the eggs were wrapped in a fine lawn kerchief, lovingly embroidered with the young man's initials, and containing also some other small gift, such as a handful of nuts, flowers, or a packet of tobacco. In return, the youth was expected to give the girl a piece of dress material, a kerchief or ribbons of many colors.

This courting custom seems to have died out in Poland now, although painted eggs are still prepared for the Easter table, and given to the children. In some parts of the Balkans, they are thought to have the power of protecting the house that contains them from evil. A few are usually kept throughout the year as luck bringers, or planted in the vineyards to guard the vines against hail and thunder. In northern England also, it was formerly the custom to keep one or two of the more beautifully decorated "Pace-eggs." They were set in tall ale glasses and kept inside a corner cupboard or in some other place where they showed to advantage. A few still survive in old-fashioned farmhouses, and there are some very ornate specimens, originally made for the poet's children, in the Wordsworth Museum at Grasmere. But such treasured eggs were, of course, only the best of the many prepared for the Easter season. The rest were commonly destined to perish very rapidly in such games as egg shackling, or egg rolling, tossing, and similar pastimes.

Until about the end of last century, bands of

young men, known as Pace-eggers, could be seen
going about at Eastertide in north-country villages, collecting colored eggs and other gifts from
the householders. Their faces were blackened, or
hidden by masks; their garments were decked with
bright ribbons or paper streamers, or each young
man might choose some fantastic disguise, among
which that of a rather terrifying Old Woman
was nearly always included. In the Blackburn district of Lancashire, they wore animal skins over
their clothes. The number in each group varied in
different places; it might be anything from five
to twenty, of whom one, called Old Toss-pot,
carried the basket for the eggs. They went all
round the parish, singing outside each house:

> We are a two-three jolly lads, all of one mind.
> We are come a-pace-egging, and we hope
>   you'll prove kind.
> We hope you'll prove kind with your eggs
>   and strong beer.
> And we'll come no more a-pace-egging until
>   another year.

Nowadays the Pace-eggers are usually children.
Sometimes they dress up, or black their faces, but
equally often they wear their ordinary clothes,
the ritual disguises, masks and paper streamers
quite forgotten. The little company is as likely

now to be composed of girls as of boys, a state of affairs that would have horrified their nineteenth-century predecessors, for whom pace-egging was a purely masculine rite. In some areas they sing a rather threatening little song which runs:

> Please, Mrs. Whiteleg,
> Please to give us an Easter egg.
> If you won't give us an Easter egg,
> Your hens will all lay addled eggs
> And your cocks all lay stones.

In spite of this clear demand, they frequently receive sweets or cakes or pennies instead of eggs, for not every housewife now has the time or the patience to prepare pace-eggs; and the remembered shortages of two World Wars, coupled with modern high prices, have somewhat lessened the old open-handed generosity, and caused many people to confine such gifts to their own families and their immediate friends.

But if the modern child is satisfied with substitutes, the earlier Pace-egger was not. He needed eggs for shackling or for rolling, or for some of the other ancient games played at this season in many European countries as well as England. Egg shackling was always popular. A hard-boiled egg firmly grasped in the right hand makes an unexpectedly tough weapon wherewith to strike those of other boys similarly armed, and the art of shackling consisted in smashing as many other eggs as possible whilst keeping one's own intact. In some parts of France, the eggs were tossed in the air and caught, the boy who dropped his paying a forfeit. As for egg rolling, that still goes on in a variety of Scottish and northern English districts, as well as in several European countries. At Preston in Lancashire it is the highlight of Easter Monday for all the local children and a good many adults. Thousands of people come to Avenham Park then to roll eggs of every conceivable color down the grassy slopes.

The original intention of this game was the same as that of shackling—to keep one's own egg unbroken for as long as possible, and to be able to claim those of one's defeated rivals. But in Preston the assembly is so large that true competition is hardly possible, except between small groups, and most of the eggs are simply rolled for fun and, when broken, are eaten by their owners, together with oranges to make them seem less dry. Sometimes the oranges are rolled too, but this is a modern innovation. In the Yorkshire village of Barton-on-Humber, where the game is also played on Easter Monday, the numbers taking part are smaller, and the pastime is somewhat nearer to its traditional beginnings.

In the United States of America, egg rolling

takes place in Washington, D.C., on the White House lawn. This custom is said to have been started originally by the wife of President Madison, and to have continued without interruption ever since, except in times of war. A variant of the game was introduced to New York children in 1947. Wooden eggs are rolled with wooden spoons along a prescribed lane on the grass of Central Park, and since there are no cracked edible eggs to serve as prizes, the winners are rewarded with toys and other gifts.

In France and some other Roman Catholic countries where the bells are silent from Maundy Thursday to Easter Eve, the children are told that they have gone to Rome to fetch the eggs. Elsewhere in Europe it is usually the Easter Hare who lays them in the garden, or about the house and outbuildings. The Easter Rabbit, who performs the same office in the United States, is only a variant of this tradition, one of the many examples of the quite common confusion in later folk belief between the rabbit and the hare. The latter is the true Easter beast, for he was once sacred to the European Spring-Goddess whom we have already met under her Anglo-Saxon name of Eostre. In England once, ritual hare hunts took place at this season, and hares still appear on Easter cards in northern Europe, and in the little baskets in which German and Hungarian children collect their Easter gifts. In Yugoslavia, the hare makes a nest in the stable, and there the young folk go on Easter morning to find the eggs concealed in the hay. In England it is in the garden that they search, among the long grasses and the spring flowers, or if the weather is too bad, in nooks and corners of the house. But the principle everywhere is the same, and at this time, if at no other, the beautiful hare reappears in his ancient guise, as the living emblem of fertility, renewal, and the return of spring.

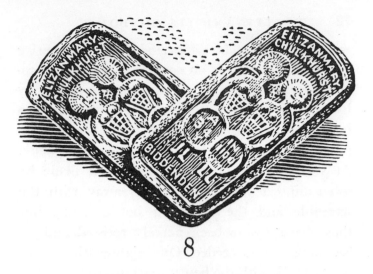

8

Easter Monday

MANY cheerful customs are kept up on Easter Monday, which seems always and everywhere to have been a day for games, sports, and merriment of all sorts. In England and Wales it is a Bank Holiday, but not in Scotland, which has its own official spring holiday, unshared by England, on the first Monday in May.

At Hallaton in Leicestershire, the annual Hare-Pie Scramble and Bottle Kicking takes place on Easter Monday. No one knows when this lively custom started, but certainly it is very old, and the association of hares with the Easter date suggests that it may have grown out of something still older. It is connected with a piece of land which

71

was left at some far-off period to the successive
rectors of the parish on condition that they provided yearly two hare pies, twenty-four penny
loaves and a quantity of ale. These gifts were to
be scrambled for on the day after Easter on a
piece of rising ground known as Hare Pie Bank.
At various times attempts have been made by
sober-minded individuals to do away with the
scramble and the following bottle game, but
these have always been fiercely resisted and, so
far, have not succeeded. One eighteenth-century
rector tried, with the best intentions, to divert the
money spent on pies and ale to some charitable
purpose. His parishioners made their views quite
clear by chalking "No pie, no parson, and a job for
the glazier" all over the Rectory doors and walls,
and also on the church.

The pies that are made now do not contain
hare, for that is not in season at Easter, and
beefsteak or veal is used instead. They are cut
into small pieces, which are then put into two
sacks and carried at the head of a long procession
that goes all round the village on its way from
the Rectory to the Bank. With it go three men
carrying the "bottles" for the Kicking contest.
They are really three small barrels, gaily painted,
adorned with ribbons, and strongly bound with
iron hoops. Two are full of ale and the third
is a dummy. When the procession reaches Hare
Pie Bank, the sacks are emptied and their con-

tents thrown to the waiting crowd. A wild scramble ensues, with much shouting and laughter, and as much energy spent in trying to seize a piece, as though the Easter Monday dinner depended upon it.

Then follows the Bottle Kicking. This is an extremely strenuous interparish game played by two "teams" of indeterminate size, the men of Hallaton on one side and those of Medbourne on the other. One of the full barrels is put into a circular hollow on the top of the Bank, and both teams try to kick it over their own boundary. The side that succeeds claims the ale. Next, the dummy is played for. The game becomes even more vigorous than before, and for most of the time the barrel is invisible to the spectators, being buried under a solid mass of struggling men, like an outsize Rugby scrum. In the end, one side or the other manages to get it across the boundary, and victory is celebrated by carrying the third barrel to the old Market Cross on Hallaton green, where it is broached and its contents shared by victors and vanquished, the first drink being given to the leader of the winning team.

Until 1938 the custom of Riding the Black Lad was kept up on Easter Monday at Ashton-under-Lyne. An effigy of a medieval knight, wearing black armor and a black velvet cloak, was paraded on horseback through the streets, at the head of a procession in which numerous young men also rode or walked, representing the knight's retainers. After going round the town, through streets densely lined with townsfolk and visitors from all the surrounding district, the procession went to an open space where the effigy was dismounted, pelted with stones, jeered at, and finally shot to pieces with guns.

Local tradition says that the Black Lad is Sir Ralph de Assheton, who lived in the fifteenth century and was Lord of the neighboring Manor of Middleton. He and his brother Robin shared the right of guld-riding in the vicinity, but it was Sir Ralph who was particularly concerned with Ashton. Guld-riding involved the periodical inspection of lands in order to prevent their being overrun with weeds, and the imposition of fines on those who failed to keep their lands clean. Sir Ralph is supposed to have carried out his annual inspections with merciless severity, accepting no excuses and levying extremely heavy fines. He was universally hated in consequence, and eventually, it is said, he was killed in the open street by one of his many victims. The annual parade was thereafter held to commemorate his death and the subsequent disappearance of that particular form of tyranny.

That this is really the origin of the custom may be doubted. Sir Ralph de Assheton certainly existed and, according to a manor rental of 1422, he held the right of guld-riding. If he was over-harsh in his exercise of it, he probably was thoroughly disliked, and since the weed inspections seem to have ceased after his death, the latter may well have been regarded as an occasion for rejoicing. Nevertheless, it is not unlikely that, because of his unpopularity, his name has become attached to a custom which already existed in his time, and that originally the effigy, like Jack-a-Lent and many similar figures, represented hunger, or the dying winter, and not any real person. The fact that his father's heir and successor afterwards gave money to keep up the ceremony makes this all the more probable, for surely no one would wish to perpetuate a public display of hatred and derision directed against his own brother.

At Neston in Cheshire there was, until the beginning of last century, a custom called Riding the Lord which, though far less elaborate and having no legend to account for it, was of the same general pattern as that at Ashton. Every Easter Monday a man rode on a donkey from one end of the long High Street to the other, while the assembled people bombarded him with mud, rotten eggs and any other rubbish that came handy. At the end of the street he was free to dismount and go home in peace. Nothing further happened, except that the man was paid for his unpleasant ride, though how much he received is not now remembered. The origin of the custom seems to have been unknown to those who took part in it, the only reason ever given being that "it had always been done."

Bread, cheese, and the famous Biddenden Cakes are still distributed on Easter Monday at Biddenden in Kent. The first two are given only to the poor, but any one may receive a cake, of which about a thousand are made every year. The charity was founded by twin sisters, Eliza and Mary Chaulkhurst, who left twenty acres of land, still called the Bread and Cheese Lands, to provide the annual dole. Local tradition says they were joined together from birth by ligaments at the shoulders and hips, and that when they were thirty-four years old, one died. The other was urged to save her own life by having the ligaments cut. She refused, saying that as they had come together, so they must go together, and a few hours afterwards she too died. This is supposed to have happened in 1100, a date which, though stamped now upon the cakes, is almost certainly incorrect. Some time in the sixteenth century is more probable, and the year 1560 has been suggested.

The cakes themselves are very hard and practically uneatable, but because of their lasting qualities, they are much prized as souvenirs. They bear the names of the sisters and the figures of two women thought to represent them. On the apron of one is the number 34, their age at death, and on that of the other the words "in 1100." Hasted, the historian of Kent, says that originally there were no names or figures, and that the latter may not depict the givers of the dole, but two poor widows, its most likely recipients. He also throws doubt on the story of the joining and the proposed operation, for which there is no evidence except that of persistent tradition.

In Hungary, Easter Monday is called Ducking Monday, the day on which formerly young men dragged girls to ponds or streams at dawn and threw them in. Nowadays, the custom is slightly less drastic; the girls are no longer thrown bodily into the water, but they are sometimes laid in a trough to have buckets of water emptied over them, or they are taken to a local spring and well dowsed with water from it. This is supposed to make them good wives. Whatever they may think of it, they have to accept it cheerfully, and are even expected to reward their tormentors with gifts of Easter eggs or bread rolls, or a glass of brandy. In Poland boys and girls splash each other vigorously, and sometimes follow the splashing with a mock fight in which hard-boiled eggs are the weapons. In the Middle Ages this custom (which is called *Dingus* or *Smigus*) lasted for two days, and those who took part in it dressed up in the clothes of the opposite sex. The horseplay associated with it, and perhaps also its obvious pre-Christian fertility significance, caused it to be forbidden by the Church; but like so many cherished folk rites, it proved easier to forbid than to root out, and in its milder modern form, it still goes on today.

Lifting, or Heaving, at Easter was a favorite English custom until towards the end of last century. On the Monday, the village lads took round a chair decorated with flowers and greenery, and in it lifted the women of each house three times. They were rewarded by money and, usually, a kiss. On the Tuesday, the girls took the chair round and lifted the men. In some areas, when the men arrived, the women pretended to be frightened and barred the door. But if a window was left open (and somehow at least one accessible window always seemed to be forgotten in the general closing of entries), the men climbed through that and duly lifted those within. Sometimes the feet of the person in the chair were sprinkled with a bunch of flowers dipped in water, or a girl's shoe might be removed and carried off. More usually, however, where the shoe-taking custom was observed, it was done separately on Easter Sunday, the men seizing the shoes of any girl they could catch, and losing their own hats or caps next day to their late victims. Both shoes and headgear were subsequently redeemed by a small payment or a kiss.

Lifting was supposed to commemorate Our Lord's rising, though probably, like the Eastern European custom of leaping through decorated hoops to make the flax grow tall, it once had an agricultural significance. As practiced in the country, where all concerned knew each other, it was a charming and beautiful rite, one in which, as he tells us in a book published in 1856, the Rector of Bartholmley (Cheshire) was quite willing to take part when his parishioners brought their flower-hung chair to lift, first his wife and then, on the following day, himself. In the larger manufacturing towns, however, it was not always carried out with the decorum observed in rural areas. The house-to-house visits, and sometimes even the chair, were often omitted, and instead, people going about the streets on their lawful business might be seized and hoisted, with or without permission. From time to time, letters of complaint appeared in the newspapers from men who had been thus seized by gangs of shouting women, not once but several times in one morning, and made to pay ransom on each occasion. Respectable girls stayed at home on Easter Monday until noon had passed, the hour at which liftings normally ceased on both days. Public opinion and sterner regulations drove these rowdy frolics off the streets of most towns by about the middle of last century; but true lifting continued in country places for another twenty or thirty years, and then gradually died out.

9

Hocktide and After

THE Easter holiday ends now for most people with Easter Monday or, at its longest, with the two or three following days. Our ancestors had more generous ideas: for them the season of merriment did not really end until Hocktide was past. This is the name given to the Monday and Tuesday after Low Sunday, two days which, in medieval times, were dedicated to lively sports and games, and the collection of money for parish funds. In some areas they seem to have been recognized dates for paying rents and other dues, the year for land-tenure purposes being divided into two halves beginning at Hocktide and Michaelmas. The origin of this

81

minor festival is uncertain, and so is the meaning of its name, notwithstanding various theories and legends that have been put forward to explain them. Yet for many centuries it was cheerfully celebrated in most parts of England, too cheerfully, apparently, for one Bishop of Worcester who in 1450 attempted to suppress what he described as "the disgraceful sports and amusements practised on the days commonly called Hok-days." We are not told whether he succeeded in his endeavors, but quite probably he did not, if the people of his diocese were as attached to the holiday as those in other parts.

Before the Reformation, and for some considerable time afterwards, Hocktide was widely observed as a two-day festival on which parishioners of both sexes collected money for the needs of their church. The men normally did this on the Monday and the women on Tuesday, though sometimes it was the other way round. They stretched a rope across the road and allowed no one to pass until he or she had paid toll, or else they bound the traveler with the rope, for which reason these days were sometimes called Binding Monday or Tuesday. Those who refused to pay (if any one was foolish enough to do so) were held prisoner, either until they changed their minds, or their captors felt inclined to release them. A good deal of horseplay and laughter was involved in these proceedings, but that they did bring in an appreciable amount of money is shown by the churchwardens' accounts of numerous old churches. It is interesting to note that, in almost every case, the women proved to be far better collectors than the men.

These jolly "gaderyngs" have long since vanished with the other amusements that once belonged to the season, and for most people today the name of Hocktide has only an antiquarian interest. But in one English town at least, this is not so. At Hungerford in Berkshire, Hock Tuesday is a day of ancient and colorful celebrations. The Court of Feoffees, which deals with fishing and common rights, sits then to elect its constable, bailiff, portreeve and other officers, to hear claims, admit new commoners and transact financial and other business. After the meeting, a civic luncheon is held at The Three Swans Hotel. Until comparatively recently, there was a supper on the previous night, at which black broth, watercress, macaroni, Welsh rarebit and punch were traditionally served. Lately, however, this has been abandoned, and the proceedings now begin at eight o'clock on the Tuesday morning, when the Town Crier blows the town's famous horn.

This horn was made in 1634 to replace one far older. The old one still exists, and was for-

merly used for the same purpose. It is now pre-
served in the Town Hall. Tradition says that it
was given to the townspeople by John of Gaunt
in the fourteenth century, when he granted them
certain manorial rights. After the horn-blowing,
notice of the Court meeting is given by the bell-
man who goes through the streets, crying,

> "Oyez! Oyez! Oyez! All ye commoners of
> the Borough and Manor of Hungerford are
> requested to attend your Court House at
> the Hall at nine o'clock this morning to
> answer your names, on penalty of being
> fined. God Save The Queen!"

As soon as the Feoffees are assembled at their
meeting, the Tutti-men start out on their rounds.
These are two elected officials whose duty it is
to visit every commoner's house in the borough.
Each carries a long staff, or tutti-pole, adorned
with ribbon streamers and topped by a large posy
of flowers and an orange. With them goes the
Orange Scrambler, a man wearing a hat trimmed
with cocks' feathers and carrying a huge sack full
of oranges, and behind and around them, as an
unofficial but quite invariable addition to the procession, runs an excited crowd of children, hop-
ing for oranges and out to see the fun.

At every commoner's house visited, the Tutti-men claim a coin from the men and a kiss from the women. If any girl is too shy to be kissed, she may escape by paying a fine of one penny, but few take advantage of the privilege. The Tutti-men also have the right to claim a kiss or a penny from any woman they meet on their way, irrespective of whether she is a resident, a visitor, or a passing motorist. Female travelers along the high road from London to Bath are sometimes startled to find themselves presented with this unusual demand by a man with a flowery pole, but from them, too, the amount of money collected in fines is usually extremely small. All through the morning, oranges are being handed out—one in exchange for every kiss received, one to every child in a commoner's house—and the Orange Scrambler is kept busy replacing those taken from the tops of the tutti-poles for these gifts. The final beneficiaries are the children, who gather outside the hotel where the civic luncheon is held. As soon as that is over, the Orange Scrambler comes out with all the fruit that remains and throws it to the children, who scramble for it with a great deal of happy noise and laughter.

While this scramble is going on outside, the ceremony known as Shoeing the Colt takes place within. When the Feoffees and their guests have finished lunch, the Chairman rises and solemnly announces that there are strangers present and so, "according to our rules, we must shoe the colt." A man wearing a blacksmith's leather apron and carrying a hammer comes in, attended by another with a box of farrier's nails. Each "colt," that is, each visitor, new commoner, or other "stranger," is then "shod" in turn. The blacksmith seizes his foot and pretends to drive a nail into his shoe by smiting the sole with heavy blows. This continues until the victim cries "Punch!" and buys release with money given to the Chairman to spend on drinks for all present. Any one refusing to be shod is fined one pound, but of course, on so convivial an occasion, no one ever does refuse, and the work goes merrily on until all the newcomers have had their turn.

Forty days after Easter comes Ascension Day, and nine days later the ecclesiastical Easter season ends on Whitsun Eve. On the following day, Whitsunday, the third great cycle of the Church's year begins, running on till Advent. The Monday, Tuesday and Wednesday before Ascension are the Rogation Days, when in many parishes the bounds are beaten and the fields blessed. These twin customs are very old, for at all times, pagan and Christian, men have carefully defined their boundaries to prevent encroachment, and invoked Divine protection on their land and its produce. In ancient Rome the god of fields and landmarks was honored at the *Terminalia;* and at the *Ambar-valia* festival, held in May, people perambulated the fields and offered sacrifices for the good of the crops. The Church sanctified these heathen rites in the early sixth century by instituting the Roga-tion Days, on which men went in procession to ask God's blessing on the newly springing crops and on the wells and streams that watered them.

At the same time they walked the parish boundaries because, when maps were scarce and inaccurate, and few other than the clergy could read, this was the easiest way of remembering exactly how they ran, and of making sure that no evilly disposed person had moved any boundary stone or mark. Young boys especially were taught the situation of the marks by painful physical experience, so that in later years they might re-member them clearly and speak with authority in cases of dispute. They were bumped upon mere-stones, whipped at certain definite points, thrown into dividing streams or ponds, dragged backwards through hedges, or made to climb over the roofs of buildings that straddled the line. Afterwards they were rewarded with gifts of various kinds, including the willow wands with which they had been chastised. Sometimes the whole company had to take to boats to define a boundary running in midstream, and frequently they halted at some prominent stone or tree to hear the Gospel read and a solemn curse pronounced on any who should remove a mark or otherwise alter the established bounds.

Nowadays, of course, all this is unnecessary, but the custom is still kept up in some parishes. On one of the Rogation Days, or on Ascension Day itself, a procession of clergy, boys, and parishioners starts from the church and walks all round the parish. They usually carry white wands with which, in these gentler times, the marks are beaten instead of the boys. Often the journey is long and far from straightforward, for ancient parishes are sometimes wide, and the line may run through awkward places, especially in towns where the old bounds have been covered by later buildings.

In London's Savoy Liberty, one of the marks is in the Temple and another is in the vaults of a bank, and permission has to be asked before the procession can enter to beat them. In St. Clement Danes parish, also in London, one such mark is now below ground level, and a boy has to be supended by his heels to enable him to touch it. In Oxford, where the bounds of St. Mary-the-Virgin run through the inner quadrangle of All Souls College, the boys stop to beat a mark there, and then scramble for hot pennies thrown to them by the Fellows. There is a similar scramble at Lincoln College which is crossed by the St.

Michael-in-the-Northgate line. The latter also runs through the Roebuck Inn in Market Street, and there the boys are given ginger-beer, and their elders sherry and biscuits. This particular perambulation is traditionally followed by a bread-and-cheese lunch at Lincoln College, at which ground-ivy beer, made from a very old recipe, is served. The children do not share in this meal, but receive buns and soft drinks, which they probably much prefer.

In some country parishes, the fields are still blessed at Rogationtide. This lovely ceremony declined in the eighteenth and nineteenth centuries, even in places where the bounds were beaten, but of late years it has been revived in many districts. It is, of course, the true reason for the Rogation processions, as urgent today as it was in the time of our forefathers. The beating of bounds was always secondary to the main religious purpose, and now survives only as one of the things "that have always been done," its practical usefulness having been lost since. Along the coasts, the boats and harbors are sometimes blessed also, as at Brixham, where a waterside service is held to bless the fishing nets, the boats, the men who sail in them, and the sea itself. At Cullercoats the clergy sail out among the boats they bless, and at North Shields they do the same, and also go for some way up the River

Tyne which here forms part of the boundary line.

Wells and springs are blessed too in some areas, or a short service may be held where they once existed. At Lichfield the procession, bearing elm boughs, halts to hear the Gospel read and to sing a psalm on the sites of eight vanished wells. At Tissington in Derbyshire a service of blessing and thanksgiving is held on Ascension Day at each of the five wells of the parish. This is one of the places where the ancient and highly skilled art of well dressing is still practiced. Each spring is dressed in readiness for the Ascension Day service by the men and women of the families living nearest to it. A large wooden panel is prepared, and spread with clay moistened with salt water. On this smooth surface an elaborate and beautiful picture is made by pressing flower petals, leaves, mosses, lichens, berries, and grains of rice and oatmeal upon it. No mineral materials are allowed and, of course, no paints or ordinary coloring matter. The designs, which vary from year to year and are different for each well, are usually, but not always, of Biblical subjects. Flower petals provide the vivid purples, reds, blues and yellows of the robes worn by the figures in the picture; larch buds, leaves, and mosses the light and dark greens; gray lichens and oatmeal the clouds and shadows. Round each panel runs an intricate, multicolored border, and above it a text is traced in color on a white ground.

All this delicate work is done by ordinary cottage people, in whose families the craft has been handed down for generations. Hundreds of visitors come every year to see the panels which, owing to the damp clay, remain fresh and glowing for a week or more after Ascension Day. Local tradition says the well dressing was started in 1350, as an act of thanksgiving for the villagers' escape from the Black Death, which they ascribed to the purity of their water. Perhaps it was done then for that reason, but the 1350 ceremony may well have been a revival of ancient custom rather than a new beginning. The dressing of wells with flowers and greenery at festival seasons was widespread from pagan times onwards. Moreover, well-dressings of the Tissington type are known in other Derbyshire and Staffordshire parishes which did not escape the infection, though not all of these are connected with Ascensiontide. Wirksworth's four wells and St. Alkmund's Well in Derby are dressed on Whit Monday. Tideswell and Buxton have their well festivals round about Midsummer Day, the latter an imposing civic as well as religious occasion on which a Festival Queen is crowned by the Mayoress, and the Mayor and Corporation walk in the procession. In various other townships also there are similar well customs, observed on dates connected with the village feast, the patronal festival of the parish church, Midsummer, or Oak Apple Day.

One other Ascensiontide custom may be mentioned here. This is Setting the Penny Hedge at Boyes Staith, Whitby, once a condition of tenure for certain lands held from Whitby Abbey. Legend says that in the twelfth century a hunted boar took refuge in a hermitage, and the hermit shut the door against the hounds. The enraged huntsmen beat him so severely that he died of his injuries. In his last moments he forgave them for their crime, provided that they performed the penance he laid upon them. Every year on Ascension Eve, they, and after their deaths, their descendants, were to build a hedge of stakes and osiers on the sands, and make it strong enough to withstand three tides. While they did so, the Abbot of Whitby's bailiff was to blow a horn at intervals and cry, "Out upon ye, for the heinous crime of you." The stakes had to be cut by the penitents themselves (and not by their servants), with a knife not worth more than one penny, and the hedge had to be built at low water, as early in the morning as the state of the tide would permit.

Later authorities have thrown doubt on this picturesque tale, and some believe that the custom itself dates from Anglo-Saxon times. It is still kept

up in a modified form. Early in the morning of
Ascension Eve, the Penny Hedge is built within
the tide marks and left to withstand the prescribed
three tides. Needless to say, it is not the descendants of the murderers (if they ever existed)
who do the work, but quite innocent persons
who perform it in the presence of the Manor
officials. All the same, when the hedge is finished,
the horn is blown and the Manor bailiff cries,
"Out upon ye," as of old, in memory of a crime
which may or may not have been committed eight
hundred years ago.

On Ascension Day the Paschal Candle is ex-
tinquished, for then Christ left this world and
ascended into Heaven. Two days later the Easter
season ends on Whitsun Eve. The spring of the
natural world and of the Church is over; and now
begins high summer and the great Feast of Pente-
cost, the Birthday of the Church, on which is
celebrated the Descent of the Holy Ghost upon
the Apostles.

Index

94